Jewels of Passion

Costume Jewelry Masterpieces

Sherri R. Duncan with Deby A. Roberts

Schiffer Publishing Ltd

4880 Lower Valley Road, Atglen, Pa 19310

Schiffer Books are available at special discounts for bulk purchases for sales promotions or premiums. Special editions, including personalized covers, corporate imprints, and excerpts can be created in large quantities for special needs. For more information contact the publisher:

Published by Schiffer Publishing Ltd.
4880 Lower Valley Road
Atglen, PA 19310
Phone: (610) 593-1777; Fax: (610) 593-2002
E-mail: Info@schifferbooks.com

For the largest selection of fine reference books on this and related subjects,
please visit our web site at **www.schifferbooks.com**
We are always looking for people to write books on new and related subjects.
If you have an idea for a book please contact us at the above address.

This book may be purchased from the publisher.
Include $5.00 for shipping.
Please try your bookstore first.
You may write for a free catalog.

In Europe, Schiffer books are distributed by
Bushwood Books
6 Marksbury Ave.
Kew Gardens
Surrey TW9 4JF England
Phone: 44 (0) 20 8392-8585; Fax: 44 (0) 20 8392-9876
E-mail: info@bushwoodbooks.co.uk
Website: www.bushwoodbooks.co.uk
Free postage in the U.K., Europe; air mail at cost.

Designed by RoS
Type set in Shelly Andante/ Dutch809 BT
ISBN: 978-0-7643-2897-8
Printed in China

Contents

Preface

You're the Vet?

I love beautiful clothes and jewelry. Since I spend most of my time at work, this is where I dress up. I have been told time and time again that I do not dress like a typical veterinarian. I don't wear a lab coat (because it covers my outfit!) and I don't wear scrubs (because they are not flattering on me at all). I vowed to myself that after I graduated from vet school, I would never step into another pair of scrubs, and I haven't. Clients often say to me, "You don't look like a veterinarian." I would say, "What is a vet supposed to look like?" They would chuckle and respond, "Not like you!" Many of my clients look forward to seeing what outfit and jewelry I have on that day. I have several clients that stop by just to see what I am wearing. One day I entered an examination room to see a patient and the first thing the clients said was, "Oh, we couldn't wait to see what you would be wearing!" That very same day another client told me that her husband calls me "Miss America." How fun is that? Miss America I certainly am not, but I will take any compliment I can get! My motto has always been, "Go big or go home!" If you are going to do something, give it 110% — do it right, have fun, and first and foremost, do what makes you happy.

Dr. Sherri at work wearing the fabulous rhinestone boots given to her by her staff for Christmas.

Acknowledgements

There are many people I would like to thank for helping me make this book happen. First of all, my wonderful husband, Bill, who has always supported my passion for jewelry – which he would tend to call an obsession (and he is probably right!). In fact, he has always stood behind me in everything I have ever done. Thank you for your love and support.

Secondly, a huge Thank You goes to Dwain Patrick, my friend, client, and photographer. You were always being available, flexible, and patient…waiting for my late arrivals for jewelry photo shoots and rescheduling shoots due to my crazy work schedule over the past year. Not only were you patient, but you always greeted me with an enthusiastic smile! You have produced absolutely incredible photographs! Your work, attention to detail, and your end product is phenomenal! Also, thank you to B. Kisner, "the computer lady," for always being available to help Dwain and me with our computer needs and never laughing at or criticizing our computer skills—or lack thereof.

Thank you too, Deby Roberts, for traveling five hours – one way – every month for the past year, to help me choose, organize, and clean all the jewelry displayed here, as well as compose all the jewelry descriptions. Your knowledge and expertise on vintage costume jewelry has been invaluable to the book, but your friendship is even more precious to me.

My grandmother was a special inspiration when I was a child. She just looked so beautiful! She had several pieces of jewelry that I always admired from afar – my sisters and I were never allowed to touch!

And a special thank you to Jenny Hoffman, my friend and office manager, for being my personal editor and typist. Thank you for all your input.

R.M.S. 'QUEEN ELIZABETH'. Nassau Cruise. 1967

Sherri's grandmother and grandfather, Lucille and George McGrath, greeting the captain on their cruise aboard the *Queen Elizabeth* in 1967.

Introduction

Popularity and Collectability of Costume Jewelry

Women love jewelry! We have been creating ways to accessorize since the beginning of time and we will continue to do so. Jewelry makes us feel good and look good. It makes us happy. When we feel like we look good, we feel good about ourselves. Our self-esteem goes up and we are more self-confident. Whether you are going to work, dinner, a job interview, or running errands, if you feel good about yourself you tend to stand up tall, portray an air of confidence, and receive a more positive and enthusiastic response from people in general.

Why collect jewelry?

Over the past several years, there has been a huge revival of the vintage fashion style, with a trend toward the return of vintage costume jewelry's popularity. Even celebrities are wearing it.

There are many reasons people collect costume jewelry. First of all, it is absolutely beautiful and wearable! Vintage costume jewelry is truly a wearable work of art. Each item is a masterpiece in and of itself with an incredible history of its' own – a story just wanting to be told. Who owned it? Who wore it? Where did they wear it? It would be so exciting to know the history of these pieces – and to whom they have been so special. Most vintage costume jewelry pieces are striking and unique. They always attract attention and usually become conversation pieces.

The enjoyment and excitement of finding new, exceptional and special pieces of jewelry never dulls! The hunt is addictive. It is so exciting to find that perfect piece of jewelry you've been looking for! People collect so many different types of vintage costume jewelry. Some focus on a specific designer, some collect specific types of designs, and others hone in on different styles or figures.

The Investment

Vintage costume jewelry has also proven to be quite an investment. The increasing popularity has made it more collectable and therefore more appealing. The prices have steadily risen over the past several years and continue to do so today. Based on multiple book values, vintage costume jewelry has increased in value an average of approximately 100 – 150% over the last five years. Some of the more sought after designers are increasing at an even higher rate!

A nice beginning—these were the first pieces that began the passion: *Art* choker and earrings with square red glass and clear rhinestones. *Unsigned* necklace of clear rhinestones with leaf-shaped pendant. *Unsigned* brooch and earrings of open-design with satin marquise and rhinestones.

There are many factors that affect the collectibility of costume jewelry. Signed pieces are historically more valuable than unsigned pieces, although unsigned jewelry is becoming more popular, collectable, and valuable – especially the more elaborate pieces. Also, many well-known designers' early pieces were not signed and other designers had paper tags or a trademark construction design (like Juliana's five-link bracelets) rather than a signature on the actual piece. There are some designers whose pieces are more sought after than others, thus demanding higher prices. And, some designers continue to produce jewelry today, whereas others do not.

The quality of materials used, craftsmanship, and the condition of the piece all contribute to the collectability of jewelry as well. There is a vast array of materials used and a wide spectrum of quality in vintage costume jewelry. Stone quality (Swarvorski Austrian crystals and rhinestones versus semi-precious stones), prong-set versus glued stones, open back stones versus foil back, sterling silver versus Rhodium or pot metal – all contribute to the collectibility and value of this jewelry. Discolored stones, chips, scratches, worn or broken areas, missing stones, or obvious repairs all decrease the value of this jewelry. Separating matching sets also devalues the individual pieces.

Some of the older vintage costume jewelry pieces are becoming more difficult to find. Some of the reasons include that collectors are keeping large quantities of jewelry, many sets have been separated, pieces have been lost, and other pieces have just not stood the test of time.

Vintage costume jewelry can often be more elaborate than their precious jewel counterparts. They are more affordable to produce because they are not limited by the intrinsic value of the materials used; therefore, the designers have the freedom to produce elaborate designs that could not be possible with precious gemstones and metals, such as gold or platinum. The designers can let their imaginations run wild and create absolutely stunning treasures. As a result, the average person can afford to purchase and enjoy wearing fabulous jewelry and truly feel like royalty!

Robert Sorrell full parure of pastel, open-back, glass stones with a three-dimensional design of particularly fine workmanship. Deby Roberts was so excited when she found this Sorrell parure that she immediately jumped in her car and drove over 300 miles to my veterinary hospital where I was working, just to show it to me! *That's passion*!

Unexpected Angels!

Sherri and her husband Bill with friends Ed and Karen Davis before a neighborhood Christmas party.

Two years ago I was doing some last minute Christmas shopping for my staff at our local SteinMart. I noticed that their "Angel Tree" was still full of names. I asked the sales clerk what would happen to these children if their names were not chosen, and she said that they would not receive a Christmas present this year. I couldn't believe it! The thought of them not having any Christmas presents made me feel so bad that I told her to take down all of the "Angels" and give them to me. There were thirty children's names still on the tree. That evening, at a neighborhood Christmas party, my husband and I were sharing the story with our good friends, Ed and Karen Davis. They were so excited to help that Karen said, "Let's go shopping for the kids right now!" We left the party, all decked out in our formal attire, and headed for a local store that is open 24-hours a day. Clad in heels and silk, and accessorized in my green Agatha rhinestone bib (purchased in Paris in 2000) – we shopped for hours for the children. We were a tad overdressed, but we had a blast! Most importantly, we helped a lot of kids have a great Christmas!

Agatha two-tone green rhinestone swag choker and earrings.

Alva outstanding **parure** with large rectangle shaped, smoked glass stones accented with colored rhinestones.

Anka

Anka of Novistad, founder

Anka jet glass
and clear crystal
drop necklace
with ornate
beaded flower
accent.

Austria
Made in Austria

Austria elegant clear open back and clear rhinestone necklace and drop earrings.

Sherri congratulating her newlywed friends, Kristi and Dan Falk, at their wedding.

Austria drop-style necklace and earrings with brilliant blue rhinestones.

Austria huge spray- style brooch with a combination of earth-tone and aurora borealis rhinestones.

Austria three-dimensional cuff bracelet with pink and blue rhinestones and moonstone glass cabochons.

Austria magnificent multi-colored parure with a large variety of shaped stones.

Austria three-dimensional peach and lavender aurora borealis, bangle and earrings.

Austria unusual shaped brooch and earrings with brown glass cabochons and brown and green rhinestones.

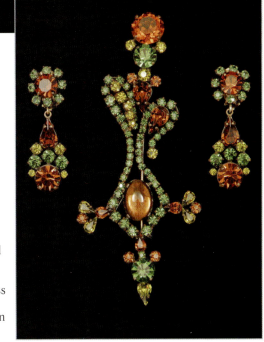

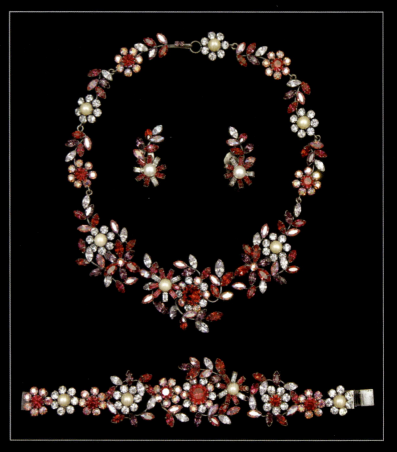

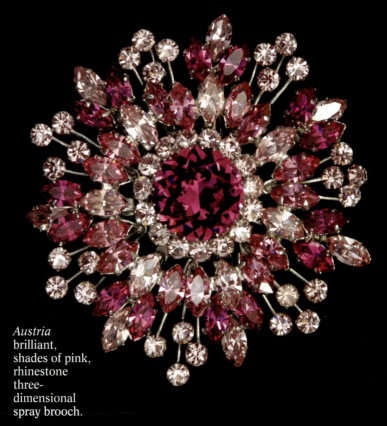

14

Austria iridescent smoked grey, topaz, and clear rhinestone necklace and earrings.

Austria ornate floral parure, with red, pink, and clear rhinestones accented with pearls.

Austria brilliant, shades of pink, rhinestone three-dimensional spray brooch.

Austria chunky, three-dimensional necklace with fucshia, tan, and brilliant clear rhinestones.

Austria "wonderful" purple necklace and earrings with rhinestones and large oval glass stones

Austria iridescent blue and glass moonstone necklace, brooch and earrings.

Austrian Crystal
USA

Austrian Crystal USA pink rivolli crystals with bright pink and lime green open back stones, accented with aurora borealis rhinestones, including a collar, pin, and earrings.

Boucher
Marcel Boucher, founder

Boucher citrine and emerald glass with colored rhinestones, leaf design, full parure.

Boucher citrine and emerald glass with lime green and yellow rhinestones, leaf design necklace and brooch.

Boucher citrine and emerald glass with lime green and yellow rhinestones, leaf design bracelet.

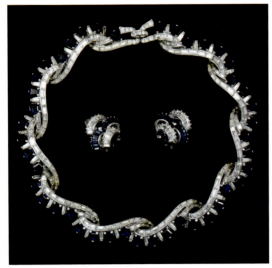

Boucher sapphire glass and clear pavé ribbon, choker and earrings.

Boucher citrine and amethyst glass with colored rhinestones, leaf design group.

Boucher clear rhinestone and pavé looped ribbon necklace with clear pavé swirl and purple bell-shaped rhinestone drop earrings.

Boucher necklace with citrine and amethyst glass with colored rhinestones, leaf design.

Insert:
Boucher emerald glass and clear pavé accent, choker.

Boucher brushed
gold collar with
green cabochons,
fucshia and clear
rhinestones.

Insert:
Boucher brushed
gold and enamel
peacock with jade
green cabochons
and blue rhine-
stones.
Displayed with
matching earrings.

Brania

Brania pink and champagne colored necklace with a gold floral centerpiece and glass crystals.

Brania "fantastic" green and gold cabochon, swag necklace and matching earrings with clear rhinestone accents.

Carnegie
Hattie Carnegie, founder

Carnegie parure of citrine yellow rhinestone and open-back stones.

Carnegie "wonderful" bracelet with large green faceted glass and multi-colored rhinestones.

Carnegie huge multi-colored rhinestone, cuff-style bangle bracelet with matching drop-style earrings.

Carnegie brooch and earrings with red glass cabochons, clear rhinestones, and clear glass drops.

Carnegie wide, bright green and clear rhinestone bracelet.

Carnegie bracelet, brooch, and earrings with oval coral cabochons, turquoise marquise stones, and rhinestone accents.

Carnegie goldtone bird with blue molded head, orange molded body accented with clear rhinestones.

Caviness

Alice Caviness, founder

Caviness nugget design parure with chunks of green art glass accented with confetti glass cabochons and multi-colored rhinestones.

Caviness bracelet and two pair of matching earrings with green glass cabochons and multi-colored rhinestones.

Caviness green glass bead, topaz and clear rhinestone bib-style necklace and earrings.

Caviness "unbelievable" scallop bib and brooch with carnellion-, lapis-, and jade-colored glass disks and stones.

Caviness shades of green with white rhinestone cluster-style bracelet and earrings.

Caviness bracelet, brooch and earrings with topaz and rootbeer colored rhinestones accented with green enamel leaves.

Caviness cuff with large watermelon stone surrounded by red aurora borealis and red open-back stones.

Caviness chunky, multi-colored rhinestone and iridescent red crystal drop, bangle and earrings.

Chanel
Gabrielle "Coco" Chanel, founder

Chanel "wonderful" early swag necklace with lapis glass disk and beads, various size and shaped pearls and clear rhinestones.

Chanel 3-dimensional brooch and earrings with ruby glass cabochon, large pearls and clear rhinestone accents.

Chanel swag necklace and matching earrings with gold linked chain, green and red glass beads and cabochons, accented with colored seed beads.

Chanel signature brooch and earrings with gold initials and pearl drops.

Ciner

Emanuel Ciner, founder

Ciner green open-back, tear-dop shaped glass accented with green and clear pavé rhinestones necklace, bracelet and two pair of earrings.

32

Ciner enamel and pavé rhinestone figural bangles, two different style cats.

Ciner pearl strand necklace with enamel and pavé rhinestone figural cat clasp.

Ciner enamel and pavé rhinestone figural
bangles, one Zebra and one Giraffe.

Ciner double strand
pearl necklace with
enamel and pavé
Zebra figural clasp.

Ciner powder blue open back glass cabochon, clear rhinestone and faux pearl necklace, very elegant.

Ciner "real look" necklace with sapphire blue, open-back teardrop shaped glass stones and clear rhinestone accents.

Ciner parure with green open glass stones, faux pearls and clear rhinestones accents.

Ciner bracelet with ruby red,
open-back teardrop shaped glass
and clear rhinestones.

Below:
Ciner group of earrings: Top pair
of clear rhinestones in gold setting
chandelier style. Bottom pair clear
rhinestone and black glass drop
style. Split pair of faux pearl and
clear rhinestone drop style.

Ciner neck-
lace and
earrings with
red, green
and blue glass
cabochons
and clear
rhinestones.

Ciner wonderful, figural
fish with turquoise glass
beads, clear pavé accents
and red cab eye.

Jesse Rhodes (technician), Dr. Bruce Crull, and Phylis Jensen (receptionist) sporting the new additions to their uniforms.

My staff at the veterinary hospital loves my jewelry. Several employees comment on each piece every day I wear it to work, so I thought it would be nice for them to be able to wear some of my beautiful jewelry to work as well. I gathered up 35 rhinestone necklaces and gave one to each of my employees to wear as part of their uniform. Dr. Bruce Crull, the only male on the team at that time, was good-humoredly upset when he did not receive his rhinestone necklace, so he "borrowed" his wife's, Dr. Michelle Crull, who is also a veterinarian on our team.

Everybody Loves Jewelry! Pictured left to right: Emily Horton (technician), Dayna Sitnik (technician), Lori Cantrell, (receptionist), April Keith (assistant manager) with "Sally."

Coppola e Toppo
Bruno Coppola and Lyda Coppola Toppo, founders

Coppola e Toppo bright pink glass strand necklace with pink and clear glass bead bow. I found this Coppola e Toppo necklace at a flea market in the Boston area about ten years ago with a price tag of $150. Since I did not know much about the value of costume jewelry at that time, I thought this price was too high, but I reluctantly purchased it anyway because it was pink. (I love pink!)

Coppola e Toppo iridescent red and garnet red glass strand necklace with beaded bow.

Coppola e Toppo
multiple shades of
blue glass strand
necklace with glass
bead caps.

Coppola e Toppo
watermelon
rivolli crystal
and green glass
bead, wide
bracelet and
earrings.

Coppola e Toppo
powder blue and
satin blue glass
bead, tie-style
choker.

Coro
Mr. Cohn and Gerald Rosenberg, founders

Corocraft three-dimensional, floral bangle with colored glass cabochons, enamel leaves and clear pave rhinestones.

Cristobal
Steven Miners, founder

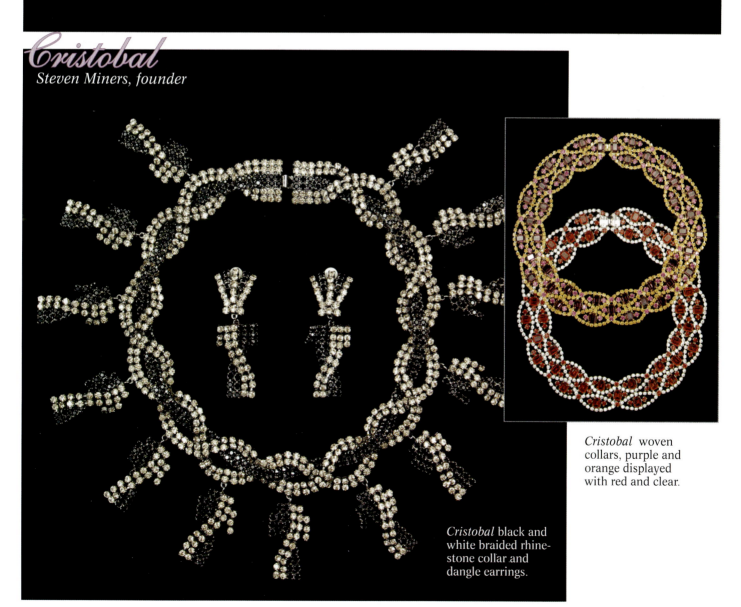

Cristobal woven collars, purple and orange displayed with red and clear.

Cristobal black and white braided rhinestone collar and dangle earrings.

De Mario
Robert DeMario, founder

DeMario unbelievable ornate necklace and earrings with carved glass leaves, rhinestones and seed beads.

DeMario ornate gold leaf and clear rhinestone brooch and earrings.

DeMario ornate blue glass strand, seed bead and rhinestone necklace.

Inset:
DeMario ornate, black pearl strand bracelet, earrings and pair of scattcr pins with multi rhinestones and seed bead accents.

DeMario exceptional red and black glass bead drop- style necklace with glass cabochon centerpiece. Upon entering a local antiques shop, I noticed the shop owner, Sherry Evans, wearing this fabulous necklace and I loved it so much that I bought it right from around her neck!

DeMario three-dimensional leaf design, citrine and topaz glass with rhinestone necklace and drop earrings.

Dior
Christian Dior, founder

Dior "brilliant" clear rhinestone and pearl cab drop pendant necklace and matching brooch.

Dior colorful chandelier earrings with deep blue glass stones, accented by fucshia pink and lime green glass beads.

Dior by Kramer New York, clear baguette and rhinestone accent three-piece set.

Dior 1960's choker and earrings with a colorful combination of rhinestones and glass stones.

Dior green glass and clear rhinestone bracelet.

Dominique
*a humble man who wishes
to remain unknown, founder*

Dominque "fabu-
lous" collar and
matching earrings.
Red, blue and
green cabochons
with
clear rhinestones.

Eisenberg
Eisenberg Brothers, founders

Eisenberg brilliant marquise and clear round rhinestone parure.

Eisenberg drippy clear rhinestone necklace with complimenting bracelet and earrings.

Eisenberg bracelets: Top, brilliant clear wide rhinestone bracelet . Middle, blue and clear pave bracelet. Bottom, clear rhinestone and pave ribbon bracelet.

Eisenberg large fur clip clear rhinestones in a variety of shapes and sizes.

Eugene

Eugene large three-dimensional, floral design brooch with gold leaves and green and clear rhinestones.

Below:
Eugene beaded necklace and bracelet in shades of blue with flat clear rhinestone accents.

Eugene ornate citrine and topaz necklace and earrings with open back glass stones, rhinestones, and glass crystals.

Hagler
Stanley Hagler, founder

Hagler ornate, work of art necklace and earrings with royal blue glass cabochons, clear rhinestones and seed pearls.

Below:
Hagler Christmas Tree brooch with red, green and white seed beads.

Ian St Guelar for Hagler hand painted-venetian glass full parure with lime green, bright pink and deep purple seed beads.

50

Hagler chunky parure with fucshia and turquoise seed beads and glass drops.

Hagler three-dimentional lemon/lime full parure with seed beads and glass drops.

Hagler heavily ornate, swag necklace and earrings with turquoise glass cabochons, rhinestones, seed beads, and pearl dangles.

Below:
Hagler pair of brooches with pastel art glass, seed beads, and carved flowers and leaves.

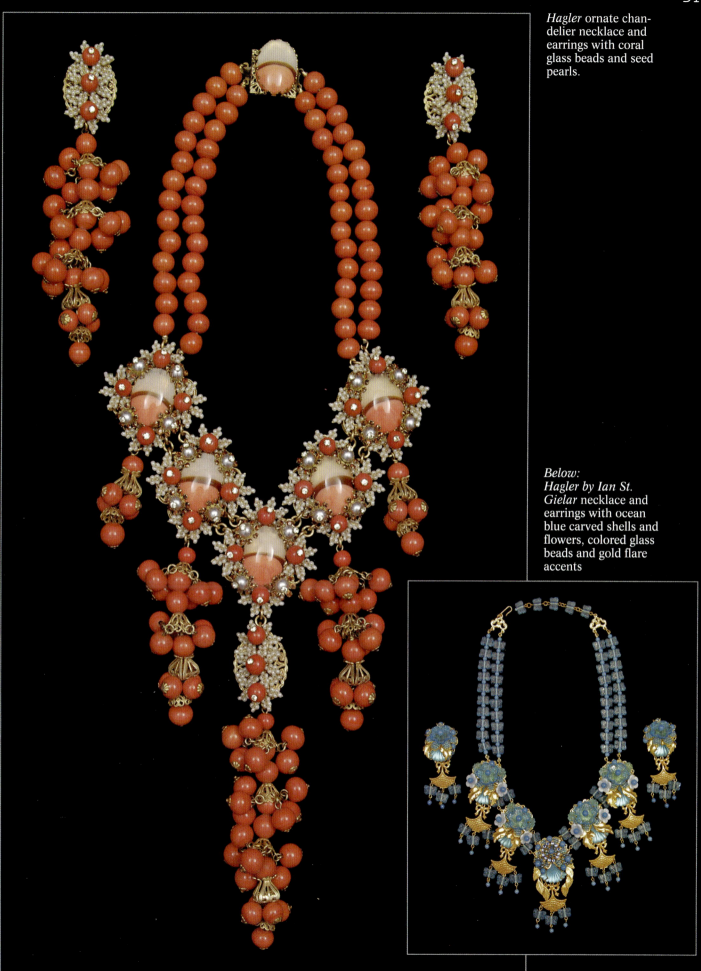

Hagler ornate chandelier necklace and earrings with coral glass beads and seed pearls.

Below:
Hagler by Ian St. Gielar necklace and earrings with ocean blue carved shells and flowers, colored glass beads and gold flare accents

Haskell
Miriam Haskell, founder

Miriam Haskell
ornate faux
pearl and seed
pearl necklaces
of interesting
similar designs
with earrings.

*Miriam
Haskell* clear
rhinestone,
marquise
and teardrop
necklace.

Miriam Haskell ornate red glass bead, gold leaf and pearl, medallion necklace.

Miriam Haskell early parure of deep red glass and pavé leaf design.

Miriam Haskell blue and green glass necklace and earrings with iridescent faceted stone.

Miriam Haskell ornate, faux pearl and aurora borealis parure.

Sherri and Holly Lavoie at a staff Christmas party. This is my abosulte favorite parure of my entire collection!

Miriam Haskell early, green glass and golden leaf necklace and earrings, unsigned.

Miriam Haskell rhinestone, seed bead and faux pearl drop earrings.

Miriam Haskell ornate, glass drop and rhinestone vine earrings.

Miriam Haskell early necklace of pearls and cear crystals with tassel pendant and drop earrings.

Miriam Haskell ornate red carved glass, seed bead and rhinestone drop style brooch.

Miriam Haskell clear seed bead and faceted crystal, hoop earrings.

Miriam Haskell filigree, rhinestone and faux pearl drop earrings.

Miriam Haskell purple faceted glass necklace with purple glass and rhinestones brooch.

Miriam Haskell cranberry glass and seed bead cluster necklace and earrings.

Miriam Haskell pastel yellow glass and hematite seed bead necklace, earrings, and brooch.

Miriam Haskell faux pearl, pink iridescent art glass and seed bead parure.

Miriam Haskell rhinestone, grey seed bead and faux pearl drop necklace and bracelet.

Hobé
William W. Hobé, founder

Hobé elegant choker necklace and earrings with red glass stones and clear paste set rhinestones.

Hobé sterling group of brooches: Top, brooch with citrine glass heart with floral accent. Left, brooch with aqua double heart glass stones. Right, brooch with peridot green glass stone and 14kt accent.

Hobé sterling silver group: Top, brooch of aqua heart shaped and round glass stones with tassel swags. Middle, bracelet of aqua round glass stones in a concave design. Bottom, brooch of aqua heart-shaped and round glass stones with tassel swags and 14 kt accents.

Hobé drop style necklace and earrings with green glass stones and green and clear rhinestones.

Hobé "early" gilt drop-style necklaces: Left, necklace with pink and clear glass stones. Right, necklace with blue and clear glass stones.

Hobé "early" necklace and earrings with blue glass cabochons and clear paste set rhinestones.

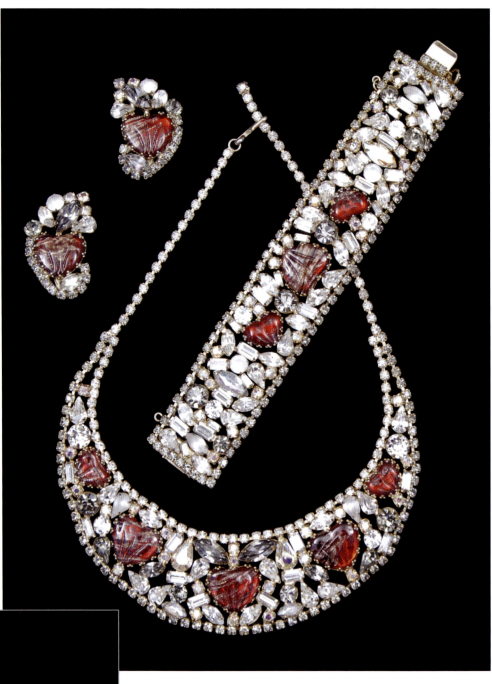

Hobé necklace, bracelet and ear-rings of red carved glass hearts with smoked and clear rhinestones.

Hobé necklace and bracelet of blue carved glass hearts and clear rhinestones.

Hobé "early" gilt aqua glass and clear open-back stone brooch, bracelet and earrings.

Hobé braided gold choker with citrine and topaz crystal drops and pearl accents.

Hobé "Jewels of Splendor" silvertone bangle, brooch and earrings with open-back blue stones, clear rhinestones and gold filigree accents.

I have such wonderful clients and receive so many gifts from them. They make me feel so special. Many of my clients know that I collect costume jewelry and have given me gifts of beautiful jewels. I love my clients and patients and truly appreciate their thinking of me!

Archie Daniels, a nine year-old male Yorkie, sent a Happy Easter greeting with unsigned purple earrings to bark about.

Dr. Shevin
Happy Easter
"Archie"
Daniels

The "Sugar Babies." "Sugar" Davis's six Schnauzer puppies arranged in a true "puppy bouquet."

A lovely Lisner demi-parure from Pam and Ron Davis, "Sugar" Davis, and the "Sugar Babies."

In loving memory of "Molly" Burgoon. This photograph of "Molly" was given to Dr. Sherri by Lori and Sonny Burgoon in a silver frame that was engraved "Dr. Sherri, thank you for all your love and care, Molly."

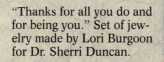

"Thanks for all you do and for being you." Set of jewelry made by Lori Burgoon for Dr. Sherri Duncan.

Hollycraft
Joseph Chorbajian, founder

Hollycraft multi-colored rhinestone grouping: Wide bracelet, brooch and two pair of earrings.

Hollycraft drop-style necklace and earrings with iridescent deep purple and aurora borealis stones.

Hollycraft aurora borealis, headlight design choker, floral brooch and earrings.

Jomaz
Joseph Mazer, founder

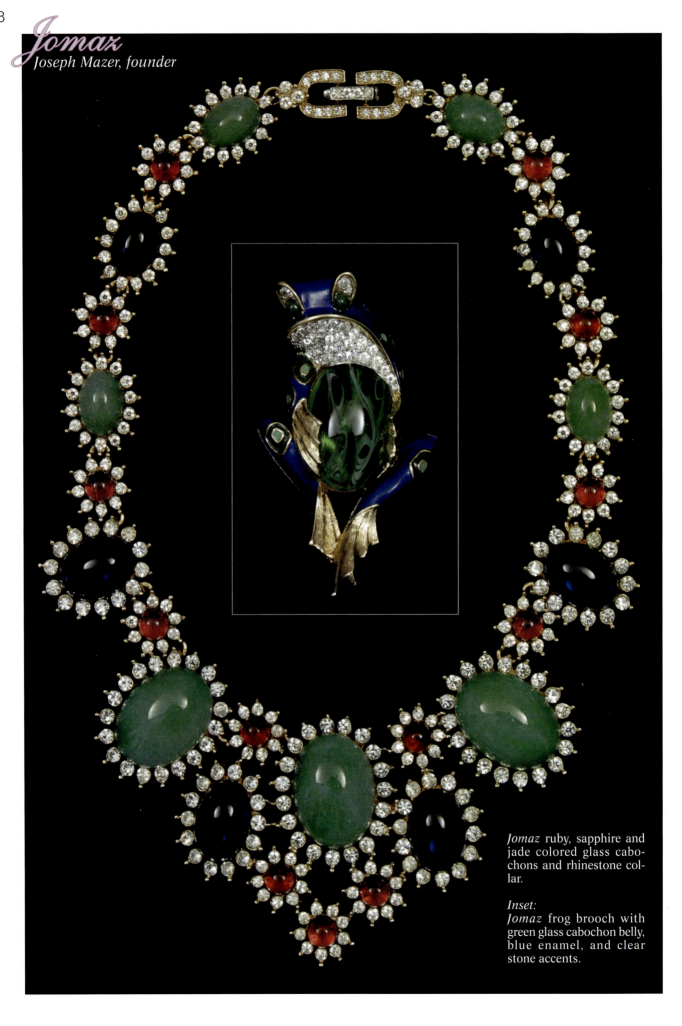

Jomaz ruby, sapphire and jade colored glass cabochons and rhinestone collar.

Inset:
Jomaz frog brooch with green glass cabochon belly, blue enamel, and clear stone accents.

Jomaz citrine glass, sapphire glass drop and rhinestone brooch.

Jomaz pink and purple glass and clear rhinestones brooch and earrings.

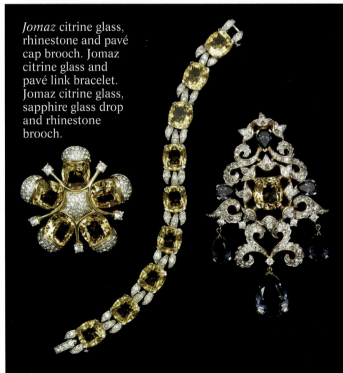

Jomaz citrine glass, rhinestone and pavé cap brooch. Jomaz citrine glass and pavé link bracelet. Jomaz citrine glass, sapphire glass drop and rhinestone brooch.

Jomaz aqua glass and rhinestone wide link bracelet and earrings.

Jomaz green glass with marquise rhinestones and pavé leaves, floral brooch. Jomaz purple glass with marquise rhinestones and pavé leaves, floral brooch.

Jomaz citrine yellow and brilliant orange glass with marquise rhinestones and pavé leaves, floral brooch and earrings.

Jomaz multi-colored glass and pavé brooch. Jomaz fucshia pink glass and pavé earrings. Jomaz sky blue glass and pavé brooch.

Jomaz faux pearl and multi-colored glass necklace. *Jomaz* earrings of sapphire and sky-blue glass with clear marquises and rhinestones.

Jomaz ruby and amethyst rhinestone accent brooch. *Jomaz* sapphire and teal rhinestone accent brooch.

Jomaz green glass cabochon and pave' leaf bangle, brooch, and earrings.

Jomaz brushed gold bangle, brooch and earrings with fucshia pink glass, blue and clear rhinestones.

Jomaz jade glass cabochon and rhinestone choker. Jomaz jade glass cab and pavé spray brooch.

Jomaz jade glass cabochon and rhinestone, deco-style bracelet. *Jomaz* jade glass cabochon and rhinestone, drop earrings.

Jomaz ruby colored glass and clear rhinestone, invisibility parure.

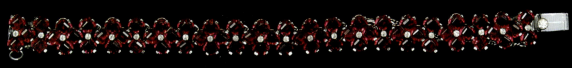

Four sisters with their mother celebrating New Year's Eve. Dress up or dress down, this Jomaz parure looks great with a Harley T-shirt. Go Mom! From the left: Whitney Ollila, Kathy Marietti, Lucy Chaput, Stephanie Chaput, and Sherri Duncan.

Jomaz blue, green and jade carved glass, rhinestone accents and gold leaf necklace, brooch, and earrings.

Jomaz amethyst glass and clear rhinestone link, choker and drop earrings.

Jomaz parure of jade and turquoise glass cabochons and clear rhinestone leaves.

Jomaz brushed gold necklace with coral cabochons, black enamel and pavé accents.

Jomaz coral and jade cab with rhinestone accent, drop-style earrings.

Jomaz coral cabochon, rhinestone and pavé accent earrings.

Jomaz deep purple glass full parure, with pave rhinestone accents.

Jomaz parure of lime green and sapphire blue glass cabochons with clear rhinestones.

Jomaz necklace and earrings of sapphire colored glass and clear rhinestones invisibly set.

Juliana
William DeLizza and Harold Elser, founders

Juliana "massive" full parure with sapphire glass teardrops, blue and clear rhinestones, and matching glass bead drops.

Juliana necklace and matching bracelet, square ruby glass stones with clear rhinestones.

Juliana bracelet and drop earrings with confetti cabochons, pink open back navettes, and aurora borealis rhinestones.

Juliana parure and additional bracelet; with square emerald glass stones, open backs, and clear rhinestones.

Juliana bracelet, brooch, and earrings with rivolli crystals accented with green and pink rhinestones.

Juliana collar with turquoise colored cabochons, accented with red, smoked and aurora borealis rhinestones.

Juliana necklace and matching bracelet with bronze and gold stripped marquise stones, accented by smoked and clear rhinestones.

Juliana magnificent "easter egg" parure with confetti cabochons and multi-colored rhinestones.

Juliana parure with multiple shades of earthtone-colored rhinestones and accented with complementary glass beads.

Julio

Julio cuff bracelet and earrings with cranberry molded-glass hearts and pastel-pink glass beads.

Julio necklace and earrings with cranberry molded glass hearts, lime green and clear rhinestones and an art-glass accented chain.

Kramer
Kramer Brothers (Louis, Morris, and Harry), founders

Kramer group of inverted, open-back, stone necklaces: Left, fuc-shia and purple stones. Center, topaz and gray stones with a matching bracelet and earrings. Right, stones in shades of green and blue.

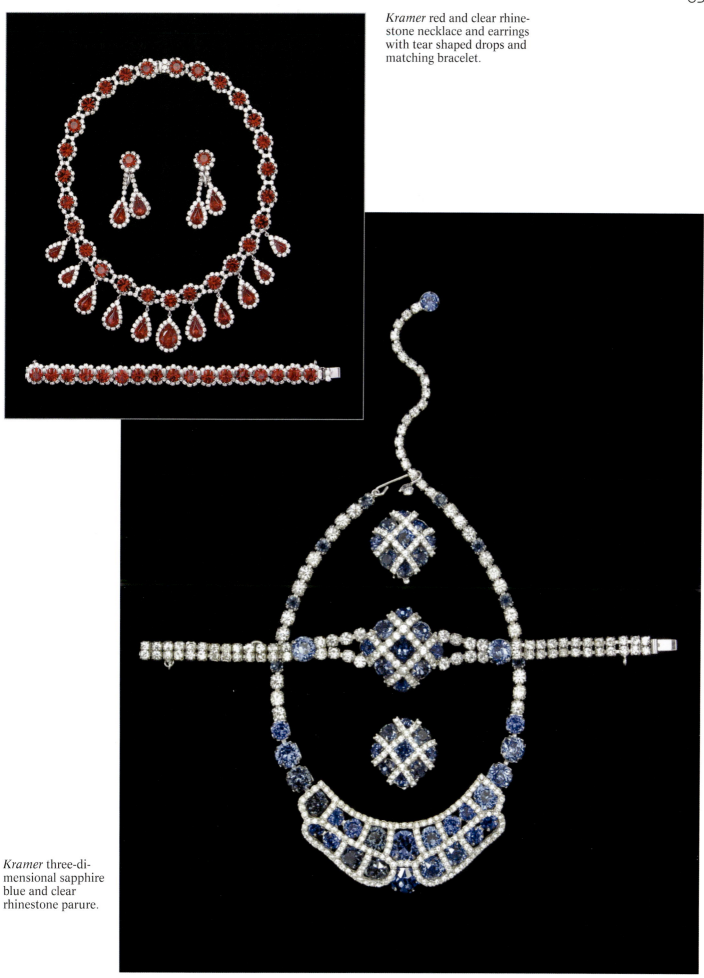

Kramer red and clear rhinestone necklace and earrings with tear shaped drops and matching bracelet.

Kramer three-dimensional sapphire blue and clear rhinestone parure.

Kramer necklace, bracelet, and two pair of earrings with emerald green faceted glass and clear rhinestones.

Kramer "elegant" necklace with sapphire blue and clear pave rhinestone drop.

Kramer "floral design" teal blue and clear rhinestone necklace and earrings.

Dr. Sherri and "Zeppelin" Bennett, a 17-year-old male pomeranian/shi tzu mix.

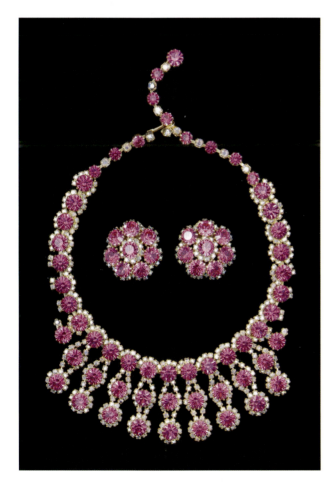

Kramer fucshia and clear rhinestone fringe necklace with matching earrings.

Kramer regal full parure of teal blue and clear rhinestones.

Lane (KJL)
Kenneth Jay Lane, founder

Kenneth Jay Lane multi-strand black glass bead necklace with a figural leopard's head clasp.

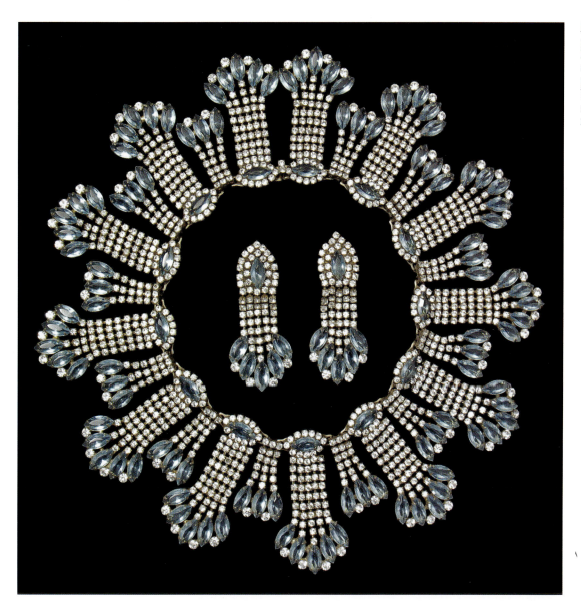

Kenneth Jay Lane phenomenal collar and matching drop earrings with powder blue, open back marquise stones and clear rhinestones.

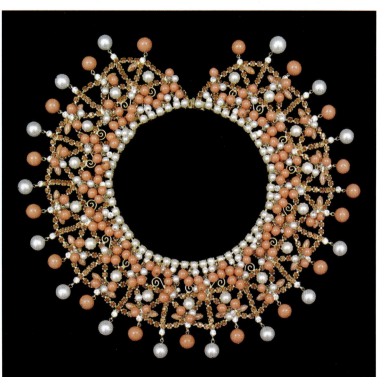

Kenneth Jay Lane huge three-dimentional bib necklace with topaz rhinestones, coral glass beads, and pearl drops.

Kenneth Jay Lane drop-style choker of pastel yellow open-back glass stones and clear rhinestones, with matching bow top earrings.

Kenneth Jay Lane "Let Them Eat Cake" collar of pavé clear rhinestone bows, with matching chandelier earrings.

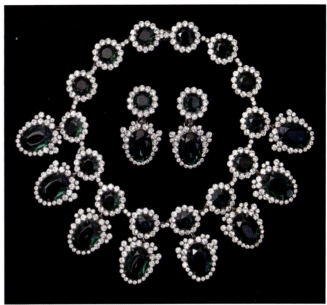

Kenneth Jay Lane masterpiece bib necklace and matching earrings of crystal clear teardrop design of open-back stones, clear rhinestones, and pearl dangles.

Kenneth Jay Lane drop-style choker of emerald green open-back glass stones and clear rhinestones, with matching earrings.

Kenneth Jay Lane drop earrings of green glass cabochons and beads accented with clear rhinestones and pearl dangles.

Kenneth Jay Lane chandelier earrings with carnelian glass cabochons, coral glass stones, and clear rhinestone accents.

Kenneth Jay Lane umbrella style drop earrings with aqua open stones, clear rhinestones, turquoise colored glass beads and pearl dangles.

Kenneth Jay Lane chandelier earrings with deep blue glass cabochons, green beads, and clear rhinestones.

Kenneth Jay Lane choker layered with black teardrop-shaped glass cabochons, black and clear rhinestones, and clear open-back crystal drops.

Several years ago, I went shopping with my 12-year-old niece, Brianna. We stopped into an antiques store and saw the most fabulous K.J.L. crystal bib ever! I immediately fell in love with it. I tried it on and, "Oh Dear God!" It looked even better – until I glanced at the price tag - $500 (and it didn't even have matching earrings)! At that point in my collecting career, I had never spent that much money on a piece of jewelry. I sadly removed the jewels from around my neck, handed it back to the sales clerk, and Brianna and I left the store. As we were walking down the street. I kept thinking and talking about that necklace. I said to Brianna, "I wish I could buy that necklace. It is the most beautiful necklace I've ever seen." Brianna stopped in the street, turned to me and said, "Aunt Sherri, you NEED that necklace!" I looked at her for a moment and responded, "You're right! Let's go get it!" So we took off running back to the store, purchased the incredible K.J.L. beauty, and I still wear it every chance I get!

Sherri at the "Tavern on the Green" restaurant in New York City.

Made In France

Made In France drop-style earrings set in sterling silver with clear and emerald green glass stones.

Made In France deco-style bracelet of clear and ruby red glass set in sterling silver.

Mazer

Mazer Brothers (Joseph, Abe, and Harry), founders

Mazer fleur-de-lis sapphire glass and clear rhinestone, necklace and bracelet.

Inset:
Mazer gold with pink glass and clear rhinestones bracelet, brooch, and earrings.

Mazer clear rhinestone and pavé deco-style choker and earrings. I found this Mazer demi-parure at an antiques shop in Maine for $150. One of the earring backs was broken, but I knew Deby could fix it!

Mazer deco choker and earrings with square citrine glass and clear rhinestones.

Mazer clear rhinestone "bow and floral" design swag brooch.

Mazer fleur-de-lis red glass, faux pearl strand and clear teardrop necklace.

Mendell
David Mendell, founder

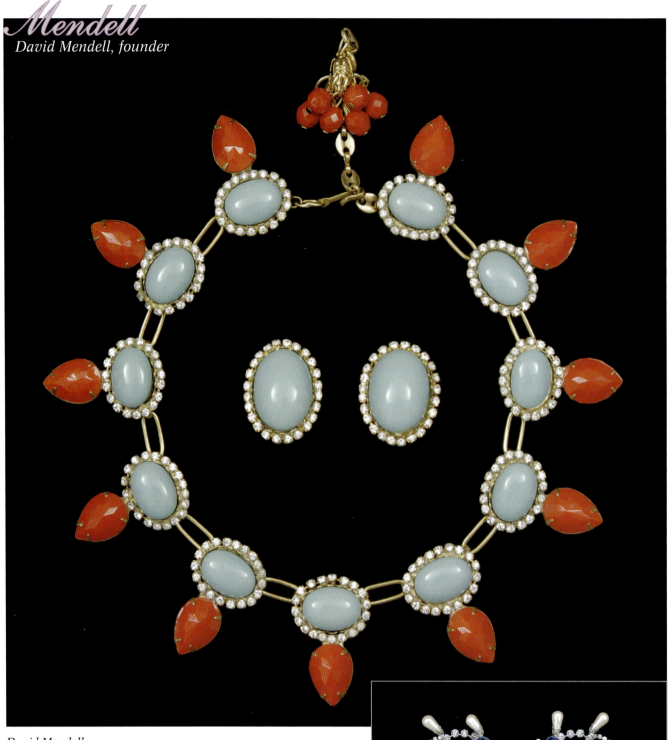

David Mendell, The Show Must Go On, turquoise and red glass choker and earrings, with small clear rhinestones.

David Mendell, The Show Must Go On, "scallop design" collar and earrings with deep blue and clear rhinestones and pearl drops.

David Mendell, The Show Must Go On, parure, with small clear and oval olive green rhinestones and pearl caps.

David Mendell, The Show Must Go On, open back purple glass with purple and clear rhinestones and pearl ball brooch and earrings

David Mendell, The Show Must Go On, open back purple glass, clear rhinestone and pearl drop parure.

David Mendell, The Show Must Go On, choker and earrings with turquoise glass beads and clear marquise shaped rhinestones.

Mimi di N
Mimi di Niscemi, founder

Mimi di N elegant collar with open back sapphire colored glass stones, accented by clear rhinestones.

Mimi di N drop-style earrings with green open back glass stones, blue and clear rhinestones.

Negrin
Michael Negrin, founder

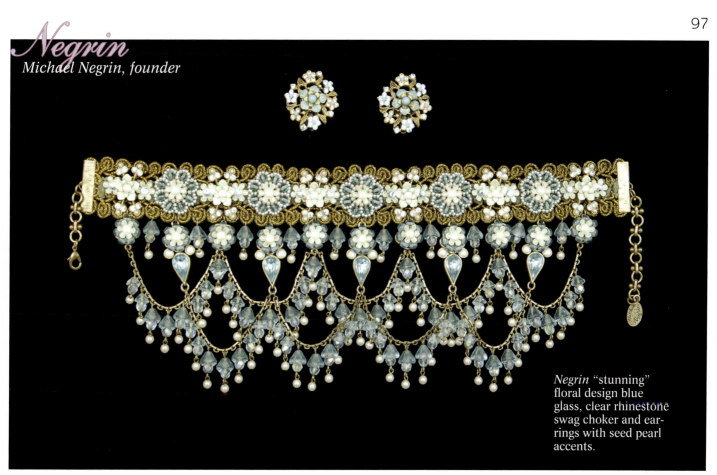

Negrin "stunning" floral design blue glass, clear rhinestone swag choker and earrings with seed pearl accents.

ORA
Oreste Agnini, founder

ORA bracelet, earrings and pair of scatter pins with oval butterscotch and gold flec cabochons, topaz marquise and clear pavé accents.

ORA pink rhinestone "floral design" necklace with matching earrings.

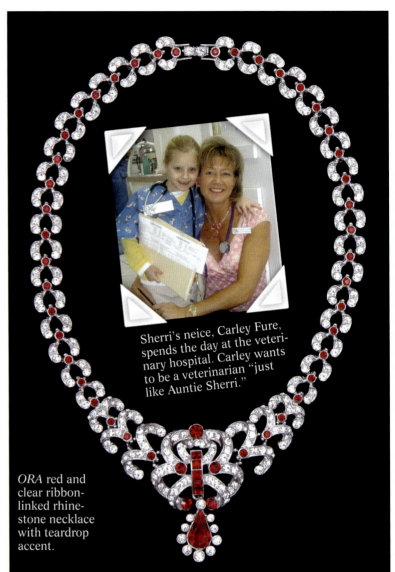

Sherri's neice, Carley Fure, spends the day at the veterinary hospital. Carley wants to be a veterinarian "just like Auntie Sherri."

ORA red and clear ribbon-linked rhinestone necklace with teardrop accent.

ORA clear rhinestone and pavé parure with floral link and ribbon design.

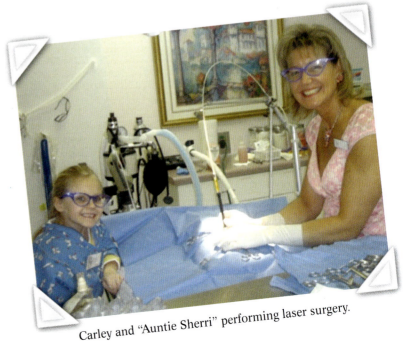

Carley and "Auntie Sherri" performing laser surgery.

Panetta
Benedetto Panetta and sons Amadeo and Armand, founders

Panetta magnificent gold spray, drop-style necklace and earrings with amethyst glass and clear rhinestone accents.

Below: Panetta gold spray, amethyst glass, and clear rhinestone accent brooch with two pair of Panetta complementary earrings.

Panetta gold spray, aqua glass, and clear rhinestone accent brooch, bracelet, and earrings.

Far right: Panetta "wonderful" peridot green faceted glass and clear rhinestone choker.

Right, above: Panetta gold spray, cranberry glass cab and clear rhinestone accent brooch and earrings.

Right, below: Panetta brooch and earrings with citrine glass stones and blue and clear pavé rhinestones.

Panetta "great" clear rhinestone ribbon earrings with cranberry glass drop.

Panetta magnificent gold spray, drop-style necklace with aqua glass and clear rhinestone accents.

Panetta bracelet and earrings with open gold links, peridot green glass stones, and clear rhinestone accents.

Pennino
Oreste Pennino, founder

Pennino bracelet, brooch and drop earrings of scalloped opalescent glass with clear rhinestone accents.

Pennino necklace and earrings with deep green scalloped glass and clear rhinestones.

Pennino necklace, brooch, and earrings with bright open gold fan design and brilliant clear rhinestones.

Pennino sterling silver group including a brooch with open back aqua colored stones accented with red and clear rhinestone flowers. Brooch and earrings with open-back amethyst stones accented with red and clear rhinestone flowers. Bracelet of "spray design" with red and clear rhinestone flowers.

Pennino parure with green "robin's egg" glass cabochons and clear marquise rhinestones.

Pennino clear
feather-design
necklace and
earrings, and
a deco-style
bracelet of clear
rhinestones.

Pennino
"fabulous"
floral and
spray design
parure in vivid
blue and clear
rhinestones.

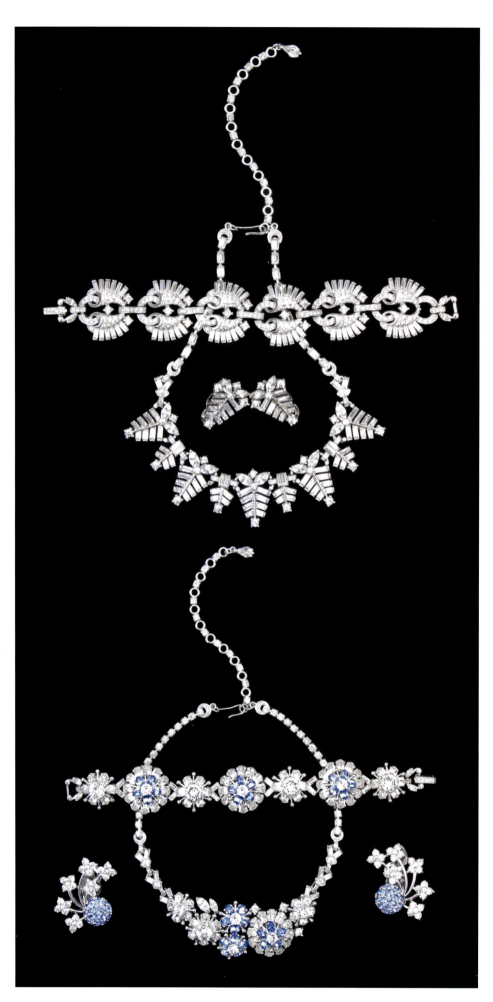

Polcini
Ralph Polcini, founder

Polcini brooch and earrings in the design of a peacock feather with sapphire blue glass and clear rhinestones.

Regency

Regency parure
of striped glass
cabochons
accented with
aurora borealis
rhinestones.

Below:
Regency full
parure of pastel
aurora borealis
stones in shades
of pink and
purple.

Regency flashy fuchsia aurora borealis bracelet, brooch, and earrings.

Regency vibrant red necklace and earrings with iridescent cabochons, glass stones, and rhinestones.

Regency butterflies group including a large butterfly brooch with matching earrings and a small butterfly brooch with matching earrings.

Robert
Robert Levy, founder

Original by Robert parure of green, topaz, and clear stones, including a detachable brooch on the necklace.

Original by Robert wide bracelet with large purple open-backed glass stones accented by pastel rhinestones.

Right:
Original by Robert chunky, geometric design necklace and earrings with shades of purple and blue rhinestones.

Far right:
Original by Robert ornate three-piece set with pink and purple rhinestones, aurora borealis stones, and pearl accents.

Original by Robert bracelet, brooch, and earrings with various shaped stones and "earthtone"-colored rhinestones.

Original by Robert ornate necklace, bracelet, and two pair of earrings with shades of blue teardrop-shaped rhinestones accented with clear stones and pearls.

Original by Robert three-dimensional brooch and earrings with pink glass cabochons, peridot green and bright pink rhinestones, and aurora borealis accents.

Sandor floral-drop
necklace and ear-
rings with clear
satin rhinestones in
japanned metal.

Scaasi
Arnold Scaasi, founder

Scaasi chandelier
earrings with
brilliant clear and
sapphire blue
rhinestones.

Schauer

Schauer lovely pale blue and clear rhinestone necklace and earrings with a raised floral centerpiece.

Holiday "Holly" -fication!

Holly Lavoie wearing the evening gown that forever changed our casual holiday party into a formal affair.

The office Christmas parties have become quite the "to do". It has become a formal event and it all began years ago when Holly Lavoie, a veterinary technician and assistant manager, showed up wearing a beautiful evening gown to a party that started as a casual gathering. From that point on, we all have made sure to be appropriately "Holly-fied" for every Christmas party. The staff loves to "shop" at my house for jewelry to match their party attire!

Holly Lavoie (veterinary technician), Jaylene Marra (receptionist), April Keith (assistant manager), Emily Horton (veterinary technician), and Jessica Stupsky (veterinary technician) properly "Holly"-fied for the party.

Sherri, wearing the gorgeous Juliana parure, with Linda Vaughn, who is dripping in a fantastic Vogue set.

Dayna Sitnik (veterinary technician) looks fabulous in the *Kramer* parure, while Sherri sports her favorite *Miriam Haskell*.

Almost the entire staff of the veterinary hospital at the holiday party.

Jessica Stupsky (veterinary technician) was able to perfectly match her gown with the *Made in Austria* necklace.

Sherri and Lori Cantrell wearing jewelry from the collections.

Nancy Rowe, ready for the party, and Peggy Bumgarner, who wears an *Un-signed* rhinestone necklace and earrings.

Holly Lavoie (veterinary technician) and Jenny Hoffman (office manager) totally following the "Holly"-fication rules.

Schiaparelli
Elsa Schiaparelli, founder

Schiaparelli lemon yellow parure with confetti glass stones accented by aurora borealis rhinestones.

Schiaparelli wide link bracelet with topaz-colored, oval faceted glass stones accented by rootbeer and citrine-colored rhinestones.

Schiaparelli green multi-shaped cabochon and aurora borealis rhinestone bracelet, brooch, and earrings.

Schiaparelli intricate and powerful chandelier earrings with blue and aurora borealis rhinestones and faux pearls.

Schiaparelli necklace and earrings with red glass cabochons, olive marquise stones, and aurora borealis accents.

Schiaparelli elegant parure with sapphire blue oval stones and clear rhinestones.

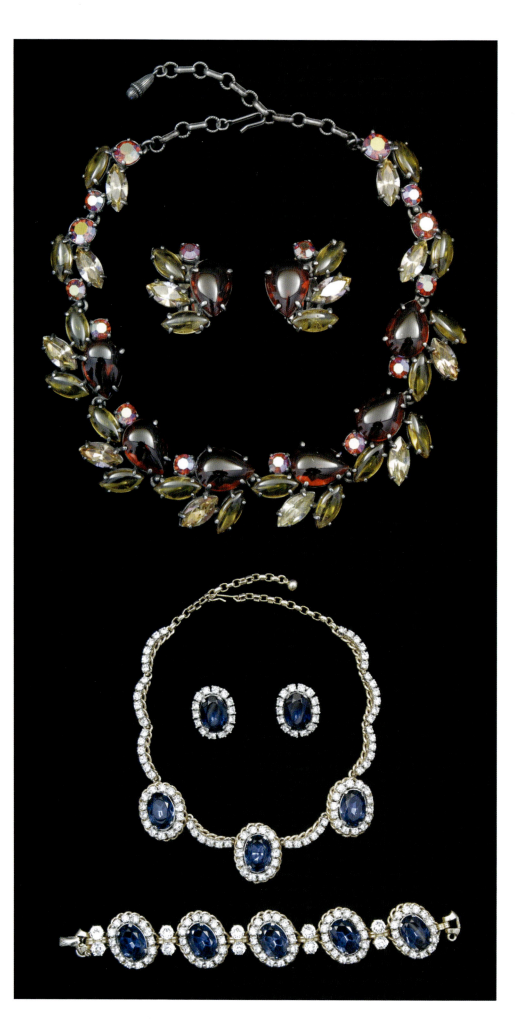

Schiaparelli necklace, drop style brooch, and matching earrings with multi-shaped aurora borealis rhinestones and glass crystals.

"Casey Crammer" is pictured here at age 20, with Dr. Sherri Duncan and veterinarian technician Betty Keesee.

Schiaparelli elegant parure with black glass and green aurora borealis rhinestones.

Schiaparelli necklace, brooch and earrings with lava stones and two shades of aurora borealis rhinestones.

Schreiner
Henry Schreiner, founder

Schreiner bib necklace and
earrings of topaz glass,
faux pearls, and rootbeer-
colored rhinestones.

Schreiner drop necklace with pendant (detachable brooch) and earrings with citrine and clear inverted stones and smoke-colored rhinestones.

Schreiner parure of emerald-cut ruby and marquise-cut clear stones, with rhinestone accents.

Sherri and Bill at the Waldorf Astoria on their way to the Westminster Dog Show.

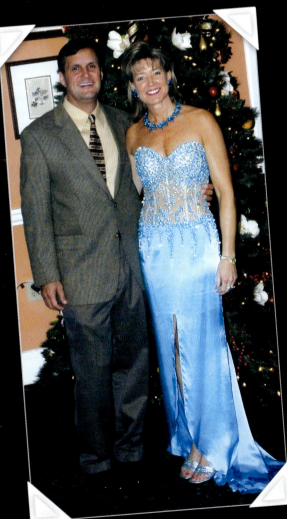

Sherri and her husband, Bill, at a Christmas party.

Schreiner choker and earrings made with aqua glass and inverted stones.

Schreiner lemon-yellow and green inverted glass and rhinestone brooch and earrings.

Schreiner pink glass cabochon and inverted stone brooch or pendant with a clear teardrop.

Schreiner aqua glass and inverted stone brooch or pendant with smoky-grey rhinestones.

Schreiner blue glass and clear rhinestone drop-style earrings, with cranberry and green glass drops.

Schreiner pendant with detachable brooch of fuchsia art glass with pink inverted, open-back stones with gold ribbed chain.

Schreiner bib necklace of emerald green stones, clear marquise-cut stones, and clear rhinestones.

Schreiner pastel, multi-colored inverted-glass brooch and earrings.

Schreiner brooch of citrine-colored glass and rhinestones with faux pearls.

Schreiner clear rhinestone, faceted crystal, and clear teardrop earrings.

Schreiner earrings of red glass, faux pearls, clear rhinestones, and green glass drops. *Schreiner* clip earrings of red glass cabochons, faux pearls, and clear rhinestones.

Schreiner bib necklace and earrings of clear inverted stones, with green etched-glass drops.

Schreiner cranberry glass and clear marquise stone necklace with detachable brooch and earrings.

Schreiner clear marquise stone brooch and earrings, with pearls and colored glass drops.

Schreiner deep red glass with dusty blue and clear rhinestones in a bib necklace and earrings.

Schreiner turquoise
cabochon, lapis glass,
and rhinestone collar
and earrings.

Schreiner belt of
iridescent purple
glass and teal
rhinestones.

Schreiner lovely and
delicate clear, multi-
shape, inverted stone
collar and earrings
with tear-drops.

Schreiner bracelet and
earrings of amethyst,
aqua, and lavender-
colored glass and
rhinestones.

Sherman

Sherman topaz
aurora borealis
choker with
winged accents.

Far left:
Sherman wide
bracelet of pink
aurora borealis
marquise and
round stones.

Left:
Sherman wide,
multi-shaded
aurora borealis
bracelet.

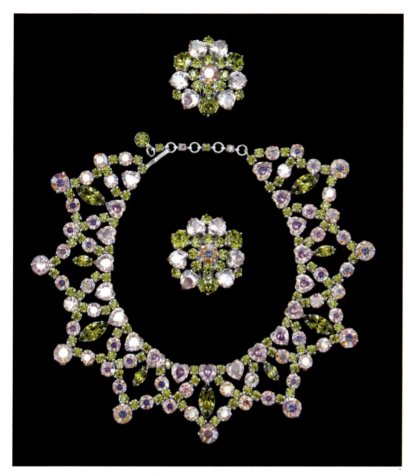

Sherman peridot green and pink inverted stone, lace-like collar and earrings.

Sherman, topaz and smoky aurora borealis fringe necklace and matching earrings.

Sherman lilac and bright purple stone swag necklace and earrings.

Bill and Sherri Duncan at the Kentucky Derby.

Sorrell

Robert Sorrell massive clear rhinestone and pearl drop bib necklace and earrings.

Robert Sorrell necklace and earrings with squared open-back, topaz glass stones accented by citrine glass, and clear rhinestones.

Robert Sorrell pastel green and clear rhinestone necklace with open back green drops and matching earrings.

Robert Sorrell necklace of pastel, open-back, glass stones with a three-dimensional design of particularly fine workmanship.

Robert Sorrell bracelet of pastel, open-back, glass stones with a three-dimensional design of particularly fine workmanship. See the matching parure in the Introduction.

Robert Sorrell wonderful red and clear brooch and matching earrings with open-back stones and clear teardrops.

Robert Sorrell magnificent
drop- style collar and earrings
with shades of citrine, topaz,
and orange, rhinestones and
open- back stones.

Robert Sorrell unusual woven-design collar and matching earrings, with orange and clear rhinestones.

Robert Sorrell extremely detailed green and clear stone collar with huge square, green glass stones accented with green and clear rhinestones.

Staret
Staret Jewelry Co., Inc.

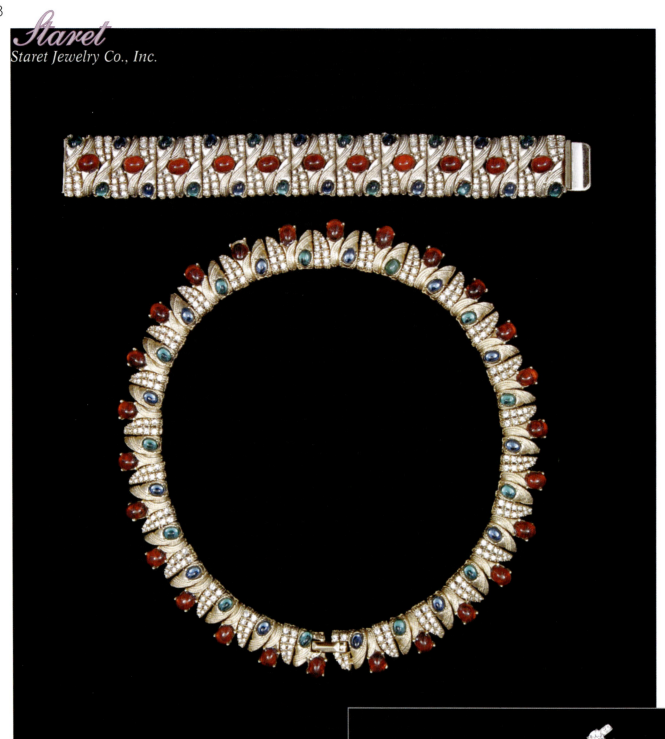

Staret necklace
and bracelet with
red and green glass
cabochons and
clear pave rhine-
stones. Ciner has a
similar design.

Staret large, brilliant,
clear-rhinestone fur
clip and a comple-
mentary *Staret* clear
rhinestone bracelet.

Trifari
Gustavo Trifari, Leo F. Krussman, and Carl Fishel, founders

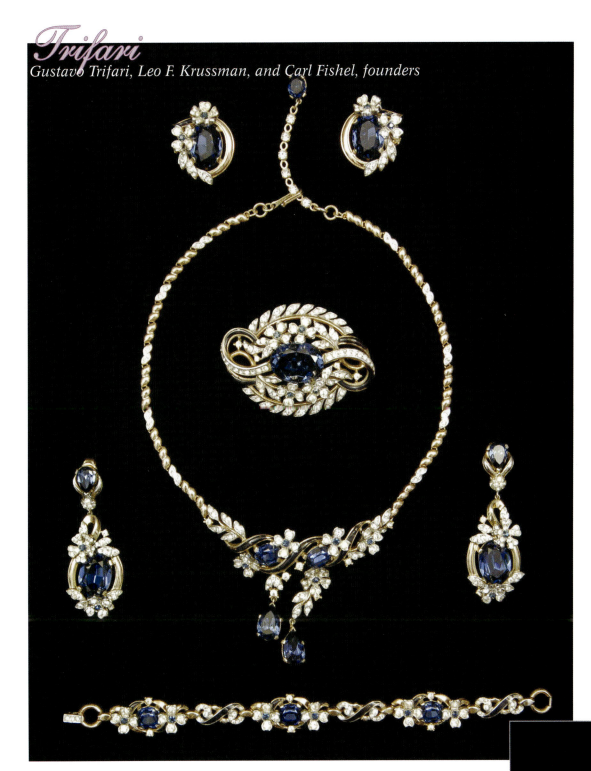

Trifari "Princess Eugenie" full parure of sapphire-colored rhinestones with clear and pavé floral accents.

Trifari Lucite horse-head clip with a red rhinestone eye.

Right:
Trifari parure with iridescent, blue, carved glass and aurora borealis rhinestones. I initially found this necklace in an antiques shop in Michigan and have slowly been able to put this parure back together and add other matching pieces. It is so esciting to reassemble previously separated sets.

Below:
Trifari "floral" green and white enamel necklace and bracelet with clear stone accents.

Trifari necklace and matching bracelet of gold links with sapphire-colored, open-back stones and clear stone accents.

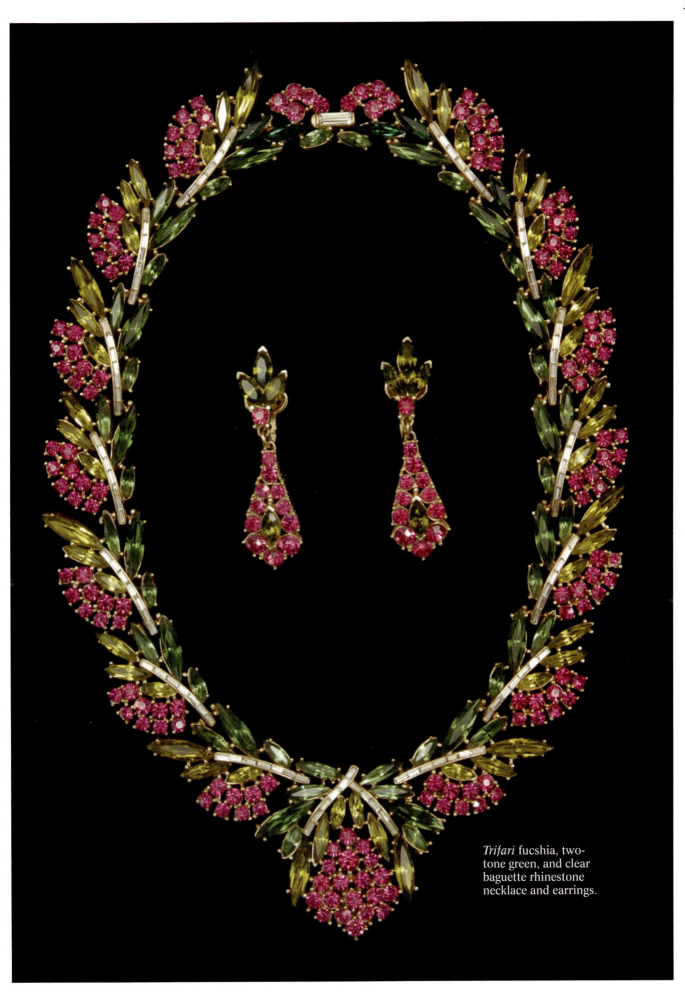

Trifari fucshia, two-tone green, and clear baguette rhinestone necklace and earrings.

Trifari "Jewels of India" Maltese cross plaque and single-strand pearl necklace and earrings with glass cabochons, colored rhinestones, and pavé accents.

Trifari "Jewels of India" butterfly brooch with colored glass cabochons and clear rhinestones.

Trifari "Fruit Salad" triple-strand pearl bracelet with a carved glass plaque clasp and matching brooch.

Trifari elegant clear floral-vine necklace and matching drop-style earrings.

144

Trifari Alfred Phillippe-designed axe brooch with earrings and a question mark brooch with earrings.

Trifari early floral design necklace, clip, and two bracelets of yellow, pastel green, and aqua blue open-back, glass stones and clear rhinestones.

Trifari ornate "gold leaf" parure with fucshia pink and bright purple rhinestones.

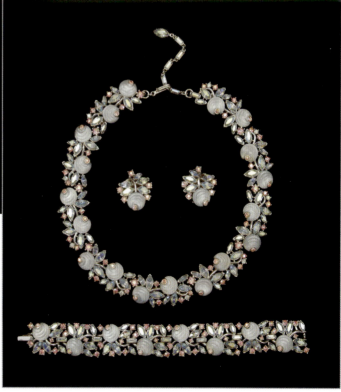

Trifari rootbeer and topaz-colored glass beads and rhinestones necklace and earrings with aurora borealis accents and iridescent, faceted-glass drops.

Trifari carved opaque glass parure with pastel pink and blue aurora borealis stones.

Trifari massive parure of blue and purple iridescent rhinestones in a spray design.

Trifari goldtone, multi-color cabochon necklace with a glass pendant drop and matching earrings.

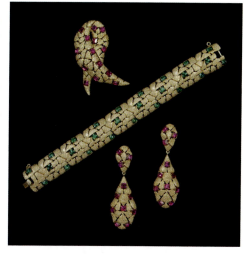

Trifari brushed gold bracelet with square green rhinestones. *Tirfari* brushed gold brooch and drop earrings with square fucshia rhinestones.

Trifari early retro-design bracelet and earrings with green and topaz open-back stones and clear pavé accents.

Trifari gold-tone, multi-shaped, blue and green rhinestone drop-style earrings.

Unsigned

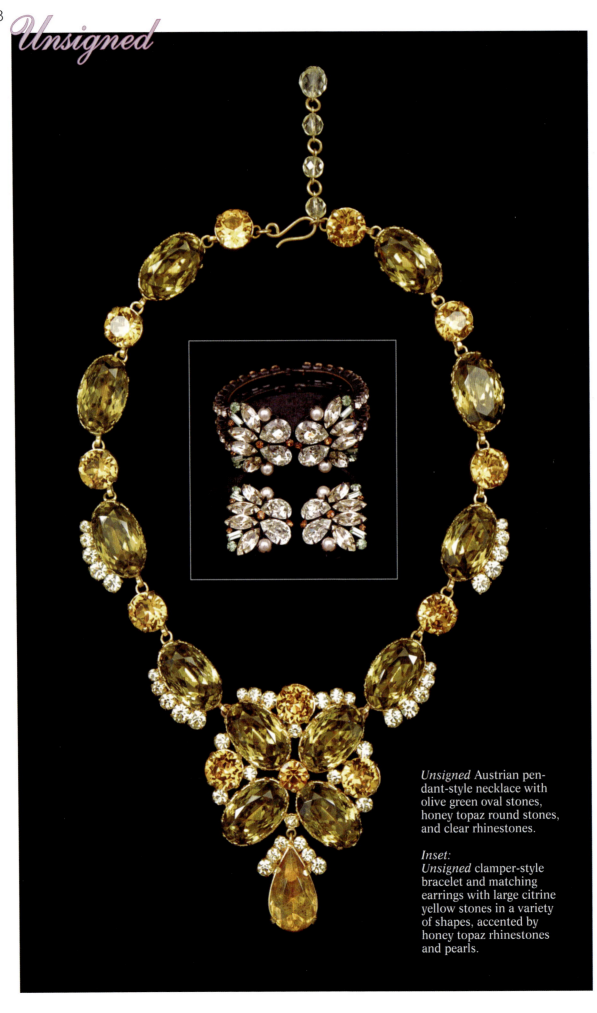

Unsigned Austrian pendant-style necklace with olive green oval stones, honey topaz round stones, and clear rhinestones.

Inset:
Unsigned clamper-style bracelet and matching earrings with large citrine yellow stones in a variety of shapes, accented by honey topaz rhinestones and pearls.

Unsigned pearl two-strand necklace, earrings and ring with lapis and turquoise cabochons accented with pearls and beads.

Unsigned two necklaces and earrings, with black, open-back, marquise stones and clear rhinestone accents.

Unsigned pearl two-strand necklace, bangle, and earrings with coral and turquoise cabochons and beads accented by pearls.

Unsigned huge bangle and matching earrings with smoked grey and lavender aurora borealis marquise rhinestones.

Unsigned necklace and earrings with turquoise cabochon and clear marquise-cut stone links, hinged with clear rhinestone and turquoise swags.

Unsigned spray-style necklace with a deep topaz-colored square glass stone accented by clear rhinestones.

Unsigned link necklace of clear, brilliant-cut stones with a rhinestone-studded gold teardrop pendant and matching earrings.

Unsigned massive choker necklace of feathered, clear, marquise-shaped stones outlined with clear rhinestones.

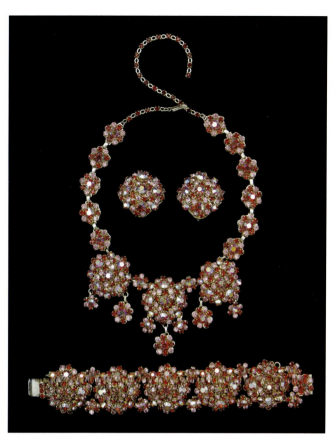

Unsigned and exceptional "cluster design" parure of vibrant red and pink rhinestones.

Bill and Sherri on the Orient Express. Since I love to dress up and wear my jewelry, Bill surprised me with a trip on the Orient Express train for Christmas. He knew this would be right up my alley—and it was!

Unsigned wide bracelet and earrings set with stones in shades of purple and a combination of open stones and rhinestones.

Unsigned wide bracelet and earrings set with stones in shades of green and a combination of open stones and rhinestones.

Unsigned but wonderful, multi-colored paste bracelet accented with gold leaves. Possibly made by William Hobé or an Original by Robert.

Unsigned wide bracelet with a combination of clear open-back stones and rhinestones.

Unsigned collar of clear rhinestones with a complementary clear rhinestone spray brooch.

Unsigned inverted stone necklace in shades of green and purple, possibly the work of Henry Schreiner.

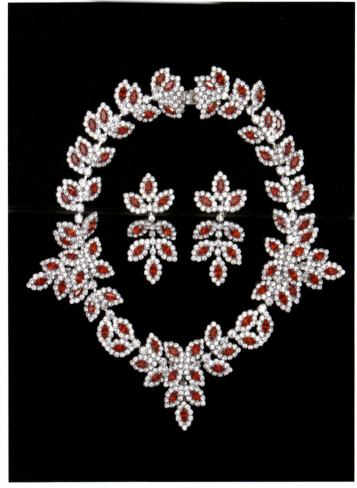

Unsigned necklace and earrings with red, open-back marquise stones and clear rhinestone accents.

Unsigned necklace, brooch, and earrings set with confetti glass cabochons and a combination of topaz, rootbeer, and citrine-colored rhinestones.

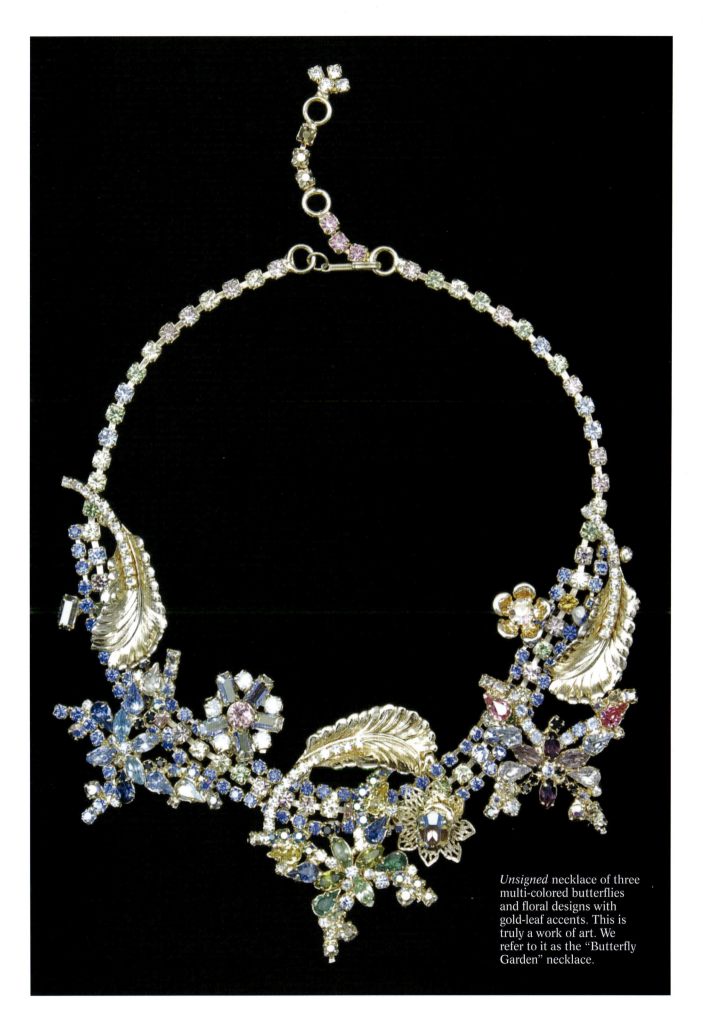

Unsigned necklace of three multi-colored butterflies and floral designs with gold-leaf accents. This is truly a work of art. We refer to it as the "Butterfly Garden" necklace.

Vendome
Made by Coro

Vendome group of wonderful jewelry with blue aurora borealis stones, large round faceted stones, and faceted crystal drops.

Vendome fucshia rhinestone and pink aurora borealis stone collar, stunning!

Vendome drop-style brooch and matching earrings, each with purple glass cabochons and multi-colored aurora borealis stones.

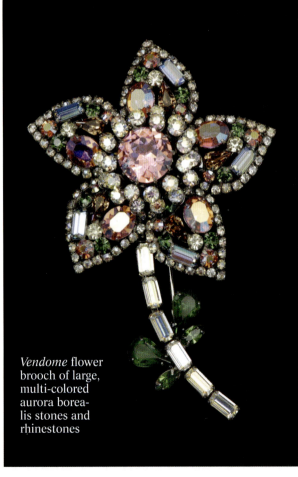

Vendome flower brooch of large, multi-colored aurora borealis stones and rhinestones

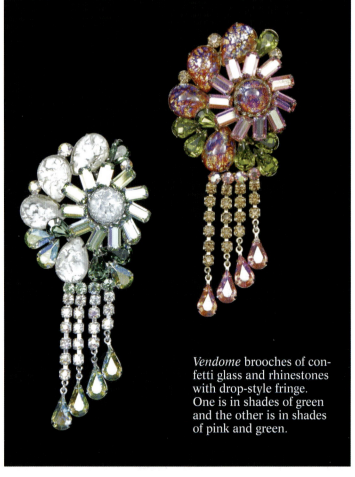

Vendome brooches of confetti glass and rhinestones with drop-style fringe. One is in shades of green and the other is in shades of pink and green.

Vendome choker necklace, brooch, and earrings with various shapes of clear rhinestones and faux pearls.

Vendome two matching bangle bracelets with variously shaped clear rhinestones and faux pearls.

Vendome pendant necklace with ornate red glass, flat back rhinestone, and pearls. This design is very similar to Miriam Haskell's work.

Vendome full parure
with fucshia-colored
rhinestones in a
variety of shapes and
accented with aurora
borealis stones.

Vendome large faceted aurora borealis and gold leaf accent bracelet, a floral brooch, and two pair of earrings.

Vendome brooch and earrings set with aurora borealis stones in shades of blue and pink.

Vendome brooch and earrings, with green glass cabochons accented with shades of pink and green aurora borealis.

Vendome three-dimensional, floral-design brooch and earrings, with green enamel leaves and yellow and topaz rhinestones.

Vendome parure with aurora borealis stones in shades of lavender, including a necklace with a detachable brooch.

Vogue bib-style
necklace with
clear, brilliant-cut,
teardrop-shaped
rhinestones in rows
tapering to a point.

Vrba
Lawrence Vrba, founder

Vrba display of chandelier earrings. One pair has coral and turquoise cabochons with clear rhinestone accents. Another pair has a blue swirled-glass cabochon, faux pearls, and clear rhinestone accents.

Vrba necklace and earrings with strands of cranberry glass beads and clear crystal faceted stones.

"Magnificent" *Larry Vrba* Collar and drop earrings
with open- back topaz glass stones, accented by citrine
and clear rhinestones.

Sherri and friends having a blast at the 10th annual Murrells Inlet Veterinary Hospital '70s/'80s party. Pictured from left to right around Sherri are Alan Reid (Sherri's brother), Scott McAuslan, Kristi Falk, Christal Fuller, Lori Cantrell, and Flo Bender. "Larry Vrba" had a great time as well!

Christal Fuller and Angela Hayes were the perfect '80s flashback!

Weiss
Albert Weiss, founder

Weiss pendant-style necklace, bangle bracelet, and earrings with stones of blue, green, and clear hues. This design is very similar to pieces made by Hollycraft.

Below:
Weiss spray brooch and earrings of multi-colored rhinestones and clear pavé accents.

Weiss fringe collar and earrings of clear marquise-cut rhinestones and pearl drops.

Weiss earrings, bracelet and brooch of pastel, three-dimensional rhinestones in a leaf design.

Weiss nugget bracelet and brooch with clear and shades of blue and green stones.

Ruma, a five-year-old chimpanzee, with Dr. Sherri, who wears conctemporary faux pearl dangle earrings. Ruma is a lot of fun!

Dr. Sherri, wearing a Trifari clear rhinestone necklace and earrings, holding one of "Holli" Cooper's puppies in her waiting room during their puppy wellness visit.

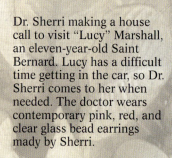

Dr. Sherri making a house call to visit "Lucy" Marshall, an eleven-year-old Saint Bernard. Lucy has a difficult time getting in the car, so Dr. Sherri comes to her when needed. The doctor wears contemporary pink, red, and clear glass bead earrings mady by Sherri.

Unsigned spectacular necklace and earrings set.

Sherri's friend, Haley Morgan, poses for a picture after a spectacular performance at the Rockettes' Christmas Show in Radio City Music Hall.

Backstage at the Radio City Music Hall, the nativity scene's camel receives free medical advice from Dr. Sherri.

Dr. Sherri with her two Great Danes "children," Thunder and Brittany.

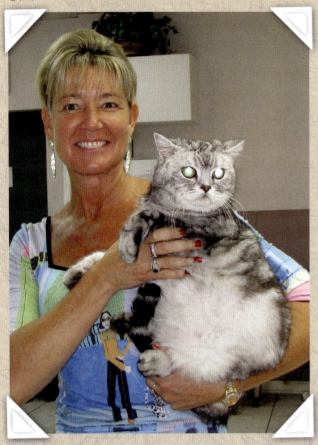

"Sailor" Crain, a beautiful male
Scottish Fold, with Dr. Sherri.

Dr. Sherri, in a contemporary multi-colored
Swarovski crystal necklace and earrings set
made by Sherri, with "Linus" Custer.

Dr. Sherri in an unsigned clear rhinestone
necklace and earrings, with a sweet little
Schnauzer named "Punkin" Brinkerhoff.

Dr. Sherri with Maureen Cathey and "Sherri," a 13-year-
old Labrador Retriever named after Dr. Sherri. Maureen
says she certainly named her dog correctly. After 13
years, Sherri has not slowed down at all. She is con-
stantly on the go, just like her namesake.

Suggested Reading

Ball, Joanne Dubbs. *Costume Jewelers, The Golden Age of Design*. Atglen, Schiffer Publishing, Ltd., 2000.

Ball, Joanne Dubbs and Dorothy Hehl Torem. *Masterpieces of Costume Jewelry*. Atglen: Schiffer Publishing, Ltd., 1996.

Brunialti, Carla Ginelli and Roberto. *American Costume Jewelry 1935-1950*. Milano: Mazzotta, 1997.

Cera, Deanna Farneti, ed. *Jewels of Fantasy, Costume Jewelry pf the 20th Century*. New York: Harry N. Abrams, Inc., 1992.

Trowbridge, Nancy Yunker. *Christmas Tree Pins, O Christmas Tree*. Atglen: Schiffer Publishing, Ltd., 2002.

Index